Introduction

Welcome to *The Ultimate Vocal Workout Diary*. This book is a complete 4-page per week, yearlong diary for users of *Raise Your Voice* and *The Ultimate Breathing Workout*, that features a daily practice log for both systems, and a Diet & Health and Song Selection diary. Users of my methods that follow this diary will be able to watch their progress improve week-by-week and month-by-month. If you are serious about vocal improvement, then stick to this diary and watch your progress soar!

The first four pages of the *Ultimate Vocal Workout Diary* have been filled in to present a quick reference guide. Following is an explanation of how to fill out the diary. Further explanation of the techniques and exercises is available in *Raise Your Voice* and *The Ultimate Breathing Workout*.

Raise Your Voice Diary

Starting on a Monday, begin by filling out the date at the top of the guide. Your goal is to fill out each box in each column for every day of the week.

If you perform the Vocal Stress Release program, put a check in the box. If not, then put an "X" in the box.

Record your highest and lowest note for the Falsetto Slide. Then record your average-sustain time. If you didn't keep track of your sustain time, just leave that part blank. Be sure to make note of which variation of the exercise you were using such as Falsetto Slide #1, #2, #3 or #4.

Record your highest and lowest note for the Transcending Tone exercise. Next, record your average sustain time, but only if you are keeping track of your sustains. Write down which variation you were using that day.

Record your highest and lowest note for the Siren. Again, record your average-sustain time if applicable and make note of which version you were using.

Record any non-vocal exercises you performed in the Non-Vocal box. (I am referring to exercises such as Bullfrogs or Jim Seitzer's Vocal Fitness exercises.) Also make sure to note how many reps of each exercise you performed.

If you are adding any advanced technical exercises such as the low grit exercise, reinforced falsetto exercise, dynamics exercise, etc., make note of it in the Advanced box and mark your gains.

Record which type of vibrato you practiced for that particular day. Use "P" for pitch, "L" for larynx, "S" for stomach, and "J" for jaw vibrato. Also record the highest note and what metronome setting was used. If you practiced more than one type of vibrato, make sure to list them all. If you are not working on vibrato, just leave it blank.

If you are taking your daily dose, put a check mark. If you are taking anything extra, be sure to list it as well. If you forget to take your daily dose, put an "X" in the box. If you only forget a certain thing, put a small "x" and list the item(s) you forgot such as vitamin C...

Ultimate Breathing Workout Diary

Abdominal Release #1- Begin to sustain an "sss" and mark your sustain time.

Abdominal Release #2- Exhale all of your air and then exhale again on empty as many times as possible. Write down the number of times you exhaled.

Breath Capacity #1- Take a deep belly breath and hold for as long as you can. Write down your hold time.

Breath Capacity #2- Exhale, then hold on an empty set of lungs. Write down how long you held on empty.

Breath Release #1- Count to ten as many times as you can on one breath. Then write down how many times you counted to ten.

Breath Release #2- Say your ABCs as many times in a row as you can on one breath. Write down how many times you made it through + letter of the last time through.

Sustain #1- Count as high as you can while vocalizing. In other words, "sing"

The ULTIMATE VOCAL WORKOUT Diary

Vendera Publishing

© 2007 by Jaime Vendera/Vendera Publishing.

Printed in the USA. All rights reserved. No part of this book may be reproduced in any form, by any means, electronic or otherwise, including photocopying, scanning, downloading, or by any data storage system, without written permission from the publisher.

The Voice Connection
Vendera Publishing

ISBN: 978-09749411-3-4

Cover Design by Molly Burnside
www.crosssidedesigns.com

Interior Design by Daniel Middleton
www.scribefreelance.com

Other books/products by Jaime Vendera:
Raise Your Voice (Book)
The Ultimate Breathing Workout (Book)
Voice RX (PDF and MP3 Download)
The Vendera Digital Vocal Coach (Software for singers)

Other books/products by Vendera Publishing:
By Elizabeth Sabine:
Strengthening Your Singing Voice (Book)
Secrets of Voice Strengthening for Speakers (MP3 Download)
The Sabine Rock Voice (MP3 Download)
Unleash the Passions in Your Singing Voice (MP3 Download)
Strengthening Your Voice for Speaking and Singing (DVD/Video Download)

the numbers on a sustained pitch. Write down how high you could count.

Sustain #2- Hum "mmmmm" as long as you can on one breath. Write down your sustain time.

Sustain #3- Sustain the "A" vowel as in the word "play" for as long as you can on one breath. Write down both the sustain time and pitch of the note.

Advanced- If you are adding any of the exercises from the Advanced section, such as the Breath Builders or the Applied Breathing Isometrics, or even applying the PTD-1, please make note in the Advanced box, along with any information such as reps or timing.

Diet and Health

If you are performing any type of cardiovascular exercise, put a check for each day and write what sort of cardio exercise you are doing. If you did not do any type of cardio, put an X in the box. Sit ups are important for singers and should be part of your routine. If you are doing sit ups, write down the amount or sets/reps per day. Check out *Be-Breathed* at vocal-flow.com for the best type of sit-ups for singers. If you aren't doing sit ups, put an X in the box. If yoga is part of your routine, please check the box per day and mention what type of yoga you are using. If not, put an X for the day you skipped. The last box is for any other type of exercise you are doing that you wish to list, such as pushups. If you skip a day, put an X, if you are not doing any other type of exercise, then leave it blank.

Weekly Supplements/Health Notes

Notes are very important. Always mention anything in particular that you feel has affected your voice. This could be a cold, or maybe just feeling a little down emotionally, or even feeling slightly drained of energy. On the other hand, also make note of any days that your voice feels great. Every human being goes through a specific cycle. This is what is known as your biorhythm. Your body will go through a twenty-eight day period of ups and downs. Your goal is to figure out your individual cycle. Over a period of several months of keeping a daily diary, you will be able to track your biorhythm, and will know when your body is beginning its down cycle. At this time of your cycle, you could increase your intake of certain vitamins and herbs to help maintain your energy level.

Weekly Song Selection

Finally, list the songs you are practicing that week. If you would like to make any notes about a particular song such as, "I'm still having a little trouble with the break on song number one" or "song number two is really easy", write your notes beside that particular song.

That's all there is to it. I created this diary in hopes that I would influence you to keep up the routine and enable you to become motivated by your progress.

Any questions concerning the diary can be sent directly to me at venderaj@msn.com. Now get to practicing, haha.

Raise Your Voice Diary
Week 09/03/2007

	Mon.	Tues.	Wed.	Thurs.	Fri.	Sat.	Sun.
VSR	√	√	√	√	√	X	X
Falsetto Upscale-	G5 15 sec	G5 15 sec	G5 20 sec	D5 X	X	X	G5 Speed
Downscale-	A3 10 sec	A3 10 sec	A3 15 sec	A3 X	X	X	G#3 17 sec
Transcending Tone Upscale-	B4 10 sec	C5 10 sec	C5 10 sec	A4 X	X	X	D5 Speed
Downscale-	A3 10 sec	A3 11 sec	A3 15 sec	A3 X	X	X	G3 15 sec
Full Voice Upscale-	B4 10 sec	C5 10 sec	C5 10 sec	G4 X	X	X	D5 Speed
Downscale-	G2 15 sec	G2 15 sec	F#2 10 sec	F2 X	X	X	E2 11 sec
Vibrato Pitch, Larynx Stomach, Jaw	Pitch 60 bpm G4	Pitch 60 bpm G4	Larynx 60 bpm G#4	Jaw 60 bpm G4	X	X	X
Non-Vocal (Bullfrogs, Tongue Pushups	Bullfrog 100X	Bullfrog 100X	Bullfrog 100X	Bullfrog 100X	X	X	Bullfrog 150X Vocal Fitness
Advanced (Scream, Grit, Growl Whistle)	Eee Scream D#5	Eee Scream F5	Eee Scream F5	Eee Scream E5	X	X	Whistle Slide E6
Daily Dose	√	√	√	√	√	√	√

Ultimate Breathing Workout Diary
Week 09/03/2007

	Mon.	Tues.	Wed.	Thurs.	Fri.	Sat.	Sun.
Abdominal Release #1	31 sec	32 sec	35 sec	36 sec	37 sec	38 sec	39 sec
Abdominal Release #2	2X	2X	2X	3X	3X	3X	3X
Breath Capacity #1	44 sec	45 sec	46 sec	47 sec	48 sec	49 sec	50 sec
Breath Capacity #2	25 sec	26 sec	27 sec	28 sec	29 sec	30 sec	31 sec
Breath Release #1	4X	4X	4X	4X	5X	5X	5X
Breath Release #2	1-J	1-L	1-M	1-N	1-T	1-U	1-V
Sustain #1	20	21	22	23	23	24	25
Sustain #2	40 sec	40 sec	40 sec	41 sec	42 sec	43 sec	43 sec
Sustain #3	E/25 sec	E/25 sec	E/27 sec	E/28 sec	E/29 sec	E/30 sec	F/14 sec

Advanced Exercises:

ABI Exercises #1 & #3 plus 10 reps of Be-Breathed sit-ups variation #1.

Diet & Health
Week 09/03/2007

	Mon.	Tues.	Wed.	Thurs.	Fri.	Sat.	Sun.
Cardio Jogging/ Swimming/ Rebounding/ Etc.	√ Rebound	√ Rebound	√ Rebound	√ Rebound	X	√ Swim	√ Rebound
Situps	50	X	50	X	X	X	50
Yoga Flowfit/ Ashtanga/ 5 rites/ etc.	√ 5 Rites Flowfit	√ Flowfit	√ 5 Rites Flowfit	X	X	√ 5 Rites	√ Flowfit
Other Forms of Exercise	Push-Ups 50	X	Push-Ups 50	X	X	X	X

Weekly Supplements / Health Notes:

Taking multi-vitamins, Vitamin C, Flax oil and Xooma additives. Added other supplements due to cold. They are listed in the weekly notes.

Weekly Song Selection
Week 09/03/2007

1. *Sky* by RA—Good Workout!

2. *Separate Ways* by Journey—Tough song.

3. *Like a Stone* by Audioslave—Good song for low end of my range.

4. *When Will I See* You Again by Babyface—Easy pop song, nice tone.

5. *Immigrant Song* by Led Zeppelin—This song just fits me, period!

NOTES:

I finally did it! I hit a Tenor high C on Tuesday. I also increased my sustain time. I started feeling sick Thursday. My range went way down. So, I started taking Goldenseal, Echinacea, Colloidal Silver and some Zinc Lozenges, as well as my usual daily dose. Oh yeah, I also increased my vitamin C intake for a few days. Being sick threw my whole vocal workout and regular exercise routine off. Luckily by Saturday night, I started to feel better, so I went for a swim and performed the Five Rites. Sunday, I did a speed routine to get my voice back into the swing of things. I actually went higher with no problem. Started doing the Bullfrog one hundred fifty times in a row and added Tongue Pushups. Working a lot on the Eee Scream exercise and starting to play with some whistle slides. Also did some cardio exercise to help sweat any toxins out of my system.

Raise Your Voice Diary
Week / /

	Mon.	Tues.	Wed.	Thurs.	Fri.	Sat.	Sun.
VSR							
Falsetto Upscale-							
Downscale-							
Transcending Tone Upscale-							
Downscale-							
Full Voice Upscale-							
Downscale-							
Vibrato Pitch, Larynx Stomach, Jaw							
Non-Vocal (Bullfrogs, Tongue Pushups							
Advanced (Scream, Grit, Growl Whistle)							
Daily Dose							

Ultimate Breathing Workout Diary
Week / /

	Mon.	Tues.	Wed.	Thurs.	Fri.	Sat.	Sun.
Abdominal Release #1							
Abdominal Release #2							
Breath Capacity #1							
Breath Capacity #2							
Breath Release #1							
Breath Release #2							
Sustain #1							
Sustain #2							
Sustain #3							

Advanced Exercises:

_____
_____
_____
_____

Week / /

	Mon.	Tues.	Wed.	Thurs.	Fri.	Sat.	Sun.
Cardio Jogging/ Swimming/ Rebounding/ Etc.							
Situps							
Yoga Flowfit/ Ashtanga/ 5 rites/ etc.							
Other Forms of Exercise							

Weekly Supplements / Health Notes:

The Ultimate Vocal Workout Diary

Weekly Song Selection
Week / /

1.
2.
3.
4.
5.

NOTES:

Raise Your Voice Diary
Week / /

	Mon.	Tues.	Wed.	Thurs.	Fri.	Sat.	Sun.
VSR							
Falsetto Upscale-							
Downscale-							
Transcending Tone Upscale-							
Downscale-							
Full Voice Upscale-							
Downscale-							
Vibrato Pitch, Larynx Stomach, Jaw							
Non-Vocal (Bullfrogs, Tongue Pushups							
Advanced (Scream, Grit, Growl Whistle)							
Daily Dose							

Ultimate Breathing Workout Diary
Week   /   /

	Mon.	Tues.	Wed.	Thurs.	Fri.	Sat.	Sun.
Abdominal Release #1							
Abdominal Release #2							
Breath Capacity #1							
Breath Capacity #2							
Breath Release #1							
Breath Release #2							
Sustain #1							
Sustain #2							
Sustain #3							

Advanced Exercises:

_____
_____
_____

Diet & Health
Week / /

	Mon.	Tues.	Wed.	Thurs.	Fri.	Sat.	Sun.
Cardio Jogging/ Swimming/ Rebounding/ Etc.							
Situps							
Yoga Flowfit/ Ashtanga/ 5 rites/ etc.							
Other Forms of Exercise							

Weekly Supplements / Health Notes:

Weekly Song Selection

Week / /

1.
2.
3.
4.
5.

NOTES:

Raise Your Voice Diary
Week / /

	Mon.	Tues.	Wed.	Thurs.	Fri.	Sat.	Sun.
VSR							
Falsetto Upscale-							
Downscale-							
Transcending Tone Upscale-							
Downscale-							
Full Voice Upscale-							
Downscale-							
Vibrato Pitch, Larynx Stomach, Jaw							
Non-Vocal (Bullfrogs, Tongue Pushups							
Advanced (Scream, Grit, Growl Whistle)							
Daily Dose							

Ultimate Breathing Workout Diary
Week / /

	Mon.	Tues.	Wed.	Thurs.	Fri.	Sat.	Sun.
Abdominal Release #1							
Abdominal Release #2							
Breath Capacity #1							
Breath Capacity #2							
Breath Release #1							
Breath Release #2							
Sustain #1							
Sustain #2							
Sustain #3							

Advanced Exercises:

_____
_____
_____
_____

Diet & Health
Week / /

	Mon.	Tues.	Wed.	Thurs.	Fri.	Sat.	Sun.
Cardio Jogging/ Swimming/ Rebounding/ Etc.							
Situps							
Yoga Flowfit/ Ashtanga/ 5 rites/ etc.							
Other Forms of Exercise							

Weekly Supplements / Health Notes:

Weekly Song Selection
Week   /   /

1.

2.

3.

4.

5.

NOTES:

Raise Your Voice Diary
Week / /

	Mon.	Tues.	Wed.	Thurs.	Fri.	Sat.	Sun.
VSR							
Falsetto Upscale-							
Downscale-							
Transcending Tone Upscale-							
Downscale-							
Full Voice Upscale-							
Downscale-							
Vibrato Pitch, Larynx Stomach, Jaw							
Non-Vocal (Bullfrogs, Tongue Pushups							
Advanced (Scream, Grit, Growl Whistle)							
Daily Dose							

Ultimate Breathing Workout Diary
Week   /   /

	Mon.	Tues.	Wed.	Thurs.	Fri.	Sat.	Sun.
Abdominal Release #1							
Abdominal Release #2							
Breath Capacity #1							
Breath Capacity #2							
Breath Release #1							
Breath Release #2							
Sustain #1							
Sustain #2							
Sustain #3							

Advanced Exercises:

Diet & Health
Week / /

	Mon.	Tues.	Wed.	Thurs.	Fri.	Sat.	Sun.
Cardio Jogging/ Swimming/ Rebounding/ Etc.							
Situps							
Yoga Flowfit/ Ashtanga/ 5 rites/ etc.							
Other Forms of Exercise							

Weekly Supplements / Health Notes:

Weekly Song Selection
Week / /

1.
2.
3.
4.
5.

NOTES:

Raise Your Voice Diary
Week / /

	Mon.	Tues.	Wed.	Thurs.	Fri.	Sat.	Sun.
VSR							
Falsetto Upscale-							
Downscale-							
Transcending Tone Upscale-							
Downscale-							
Full Voice Upscale-							
Downscale-							
Vibrato Pitch, Larynx Stomach, Jaw							
Non-Vocal (Bullfrogs, Tongue Pushups)							
Advanced (Scream, Grit, Growl Whistle)							
Daily Dose							

Ultimate Breathing Workout Diary
Week / /

	Mon.	Tues.	Wed.	Thurs.	Fri.	Sat.	Sun.
Abdominal Release #1							
Abdominal Release #2							
Breath Capacity #1							
Breath Capacity #2							
Breath Release #1							
Breath Release #2							
Sustain #1							
Sustain #2							
Sustain #3							

Advanced Exercises:

Diet & Health
Week / /

	Mon.	Tues.	Wed.	Thurs.	Fri.	Sat.	Sun.
Cardio Jogging/ Swimming/ Rebounding/ Etc.							
Situps							
Yoga Flowfit/ Ashtanga/ 5 rites/ etc.							
Other Forms of Exercise							

Weekly Supplements / Health Notes:

Weekly Song Selection
Week / /

1. _____

2. _____

3. _____

4. _____

5. _____

NOTES:

Raise Your Voice Diary
Week / /

	Mon.	Tues.	Wed.	Thurs.	Fri.	Sat.	Sun.
VSR							
Falsetto Upscale-							
Downscale-							
Transcending Tone Upscale-							
Downscale-							
Full Voice Upscale-							
Downscale-							
Vibrato Pitch, Larynx Stomach, Jaw							
Non-Vocal (Bullfrogs, Tongue Pushups							
Advanced (Scream, Grit, Growl Whistle)							
Daily Dose							

Ultimate Breathing Workout Diary
Week / /

	Mon.	Tues.	Wed.	Thurs.	Fri.	Sat.	Sun.
Abdominal Release #1							
Abdominal Release #2							
Breath Capacity #1							
Breath Capacity #2							
Breath Release #1							
Breath Release #2							
Sustain #1							
Sustain #2							
Sustain #3							

Advanced Exercises:

Diet & Health
Week / /

	Mon.	Tues.	Wed.	Thurs.	Fri.	Sat.	Sun.
Cardio Jogging/ Swimming/ Rebounding/ Etc.							
Situps							
Yoga Flowfit/ Ashtanga/ 5 rites/ etc.							
Other Forms of Exercise							

Weekly Supplements / Health Notes:

Weekly Song Selection
Week / /

1.
2.
3.
4.
5.

NOTES:

Raise Your Voice Diary
Week / /

	Mon.	Tues.	Wed.	Thurs.	Fri.	Sat.	Sun.
VSR							
Falsetto Upscale-							
Downscale-							
Transcending Tone Upscale-							
Downscale-							
Full Voice Upscale-							
Downscale-							
Vibrato Pitch, Larynx Stomach, Jaw							
Non-Vocal (Bullfrogs, Tongue Pushups)							
Advanced (Scream, Grit, Growl Whistle)							
Daily Dose							

Ultimate Breathing Workout Diary
Week / /

	Mon.	Tues.	Wed.	Thurs.	Fri.	Sat.	Sun.
Abdominal Release #1							
Abdominal Release #2							
Breath Capacity #1							
Breath Capacity #2							
Breath Release #1							
Breath Release #2							
Sustain #1							
Sustain #2							
Sustain #3							

Advanced Exercises:

_____
_____
_____
_____

Diet & Health
Week / /

	Mon.	Tues.	Wed.	Thurs.	Fri.	Sat.	Sun.
Cardio Jogging/ Swimming/ Rebounding/ Etc.							
Situps							
Yoga Flowfit/ Ashtanga/ 5 rites/ etc.							
Other Forms of Exercise							

Weekly Supplements / Health Notes:

Weekly Song Selection
Week / /

1.
2.
3.
4.
5.

NOTES:

Raise Your Voice Diary
Week / /

	Mon.	Tues.	Wed.	Thurs.	Fri.	Sat.	Sun.
VSR							
Falsetto Upscale-							
Downscale-							
Transcending Tone Upscale-							
Downscale-							
Full Voice Upscale-							
Downscale-							
Vibrato Pitch, Larynx Stomach, Jaw							
Non-Vocal (Bullfrogs, Tongue Pushups)							
Advanced (Scream, Grit, Growl Whistle)							
Daily Dose							

Ultimate Breathing Workout Diary
Week / /

	Mon.	Tues.	Wed.	Thurs.	Fri.	Sat.	Sun.
Abdominal Release #1							
Abdominal Release #2							
Breath Capacity #1							
Breath Capacity #2							
Breath Release #1							
Breath Release #2							
Sustain #1							
Sustain #2							
Sustain #3							

Advanced Exercises:

Diet & Health
Week / /

	Mon.	Tues.	Wed.	Thurs.	Fri.	Sat.	Sun.
Cardio Jogging/ Swimming/ Rebounding/ Etc.							
Situps							
Yoga Flowfit/ Ashtanga/ 5 rites/ etc.							
Other Forms of Exercise							

Weekly Supplements / Health Notes:

The Ultimate Vocal Workout Diary

Weekly Song Selection
Week / /

1.
2.
3.
4.
5.

NOTES:

Raise Your Voice Diary
Week / /

	Mon.	Tues.	Wed.	Thurs.	Fri.	Sat.	Sun.
VSR							
Falsetto Upscale-							
Downscale-							
Transcending Tone Upscale-							
Downscale-							
Full Voice Upscale-							
Downscale-							
Vibrato Pitch, Larynx Stomach, Jaw							
Non-Vocal (Bullfrogs, Tongue Pushups)							
Advanced (Scream, Grit, Growl Whistle)							
Daily Dose							

Ultimate Breathing Workout Diary
Week   /   /

	Mon.	Tues.	Wed.	Thurs.	Fri.	Sat.	Sun.
Abdominal Release #1							
Abdominal Release #2							
Breath Capacity #1							
Breath Capacity #2							
Breath Release #1							
Breath Release #2							
Sustain #1							
Sustain #2							
Sustain #3							

Advanced Exercises:

Diet & Health
Week / /

	Mon.	Tues.	Wed.	Thurs.	Fri.	Sat.	Sun.
Cardio Jogging/ Swimming/ Rebounding/ Etc.							
Situps							
Yoga Flowfit/ Ashtanga/ 5 rites/ etc.							
Other Forms of Exercise							

Weekly Supplements / Health Notes:

Weekly Song Selection
Week / /

1.
2.
3.
4.
5.

NOTES:

Raise Your Voice Diary
Week / /

	Mon.	Tues.	Wed.	Thurs.	Fri.	Sat.	Sun.
VSR							
Falsetto Upscale-							
Downscale-							
Transcending Tone Upscale-							
Downscale-							
Full Voice Upscale-							
Downscale-							
Vibrato Pitch, Larynx Stomach, Jaw							
Non-Vocal (Bullfrogs, Tongue Pushups							
Advanced (Scream, Grit, Growl Whistle)							
Daily Dose							

… The Ultimate Vocal Workout Diary

Ultimate Breathing Workout Diary
Week   /   /

	Mon.	Tues.	Wed.	Thurs.	Fri.	Sat.	Sun.
Abdominal Release #1							
Abdominal Release #2							
Breath Capacity #1							
Breath Capacity #2							
Breath Release #1							
Breath Release #2							
Sustain #1							
Sustain #2							
Sustain #3							

Advanced Exercises:

_____
_____
_____
_____

Diet & Health
Week   /   /

	Mon.	Tues.	Wed.	Thurs.	Fri.	Sat.	Sun.
Cardio Jogging/ Swimming/ Rebounding/ Etc.							
Situps							
Yoga Flowfit/ Ashtanga/ 5 rites/ etc.							
Other Forms of Exercise							

Weekly Supplements / Health Notes:

The Ultimate Vocal Workout Diary

Weekly Song Selection
Week   /   /

1.
2.
3.
4.
5.

NOTES:

Raise Your Voice Diary
Week / /

	Mon.	Tues.	Wed.	Thurs.	Fri.	Sat.	Sun.
VSR							
Falsetto Upscale-							
Downscale-							
Transcending Tone Upscale-							
Downscale-							
Full Voice Upscale-							
Downscale-							
Vibrato Pitch, Larynx Stomach, Jaw							
Non-Vocal (Bullfrogs, Tongue Pushups)							
Advanced (Scream, Grit, Growl Whistle)							
Daily Dose							

Ultimate Breathing Workout Diary
Week / /

	Mon.	Tues.	Wed.	Thurs.	Fri.	Sat.	Sun.
Abdominal Release #1							
Abdominal Release #2							
Breath Capacity #1							
Breath Capacity #2							
Breath Release #1							
Breath Release #2							
Sustain #1							
Sustain #2							
Sustain #3							

Advanced Exercises:

Diet & Health
Week / /

	Mon.	Tues.	Wed.	Thurs.	Fri.	Sat.	Sun.
Cardio Jogging/ Swimming/ Rebounding/ Etc.							
Situps							
Yoga Flowfit/ Ashtanga/ 5 rites/ etc.							
Other Forms of Exercise							

Weekly Supplements / Health Notes:

Weekly Song Selection

Week / /

1.
2.
3.
4.
5.

NOTES:

Raise Your Voice Diary
Week / /

	Mon.	Tues.	Wed.	Thurs.	Fri.	Sat.	Sun.
VSR							
Falsetto Upscale-							
Downscale-							
Transcending Tone Upscale-							
Downscale-							
Full Voice Upscale-							
Downscale-							
Vibrato Pitch, Larynx Stomach, Jaw							
Non-Vocal (Bullfrogs, Tongue Pushups)							
Advanced (Scream, Grit, Growl Whistle)							
Daily Dose							

Ultimate Breathing Workout Diary
Week   /   /

	Mon.	Tues.	Wed.	Thurs.	Fri.	Sat.	Sun.
Abdominal Release #1							
Abdominal Release #2							
Breath Capacity #1							
Breath Capacity #2							
Breath Release #1							
Breath Release #2							
Sustain #1							
Sustain #2							
Sustain #3							

Advanced Exercises:

Diet & Health
Week / /

	Mon.	Tues.	Wed.	Thurs.	Fri.	Sat.	Sun.
Cardio Jogging/ Swimming/ Rebounding/ Etc.							
Situps							
Yoga Flowfit/ Ashtanga/ 5 rites/ etc.							
Other Forms of Exercise							

Weekly Supplements / Health Notes:

_____
_____
_____
_____
_____
_____
_____
_____
_____
_____
_____
_____

Weekly Song Selection
Week   /   /

1.

2.

3.

4.

5.

NOTES:

Raise Your Voice Diary
Week / /

	Mon.	Tues.	Wed.	Thurs.	Fri.	Sat.	Sun.
VSR							
Falsetto Upscale-							
Downscale-							
Transcending Tone Upscale-							
Downscale-							
Full Voice Upscale-							
Downscale-							
Vibrato Pitch, Larynx Stomach, Jaw							
Non-Vocal (Bullfrogs, Tongue Pushups)							
Advanced (Scream, Grit, Growl Whistle)							
Daily Dose							

Ultimate Breathing Workout Diary
Week / /

	Mon.	Tues.	Wed.	Thurs.	Fri.	Sat.	Sun.
Abdominal Release #1							
Abdominal Release #2							
Breath Capacity #1							
Breath Capacity #2							
Breath Release #1							
Breath Release #2							
Sustain #1							
Sustain #2							
Sustain #3							

Advanced Exercises:

Diet & Health
Week / /

	Mon.	Tues.	Wed.	Thurs.	Fri.	Sat.	Sun.
Cardio Jogging/ Swimming/ Rebounding/ Etc.							
Situps							
Yoga Flowfit/ Ashtanga/ 5 rites/ etc.							
Other Forms of Exercise							

Weekly Supplements / Health Notes:

Weekly Song Selection
Week / /

1.
2.
3.
4.
5.

NOTES:

Raise Your Voice Diary
Week / /

	Mon.	Tues.	Wed.	Thurs.	Fri.	Sat.	Sun.
VSR							
Falsetto Upscale-							
Downscale-							
Transcending Tone Upscale-							
Downscale-							
Full Voice Upscale-							
Downscale-							
Vibrato Pitch, Larynx Stomach, Jaw							
Non-Vocal (Bullfrogs, Tongue Pushups)							
Advanced (Scream, Grit, Growl Whistle)							
Daily Dose							

Ultimate Breathing Workout Diary
Week / /

	Mon.	Tues.	Wed.	Thurs.	Fri.	Sat.	Sun.
Abdominal Release #1							
Abdominal Release #2							
Breath Capacity #1							
Breath Capacity #2							
Breath Release #1							
Breath Release #2							
Sustain #1							
Sustain #2							
Sustain #3							

Advanced Exercises:

Diet & Health
Week / /

	Mon.	Tues.	Wed.	Thurs.	Fri.	Sat.	Sun.
Cardio Jogging/ Swimming/ Rebounding/ Etc.							
Situps							
Yoga Flowfit/ Ashtanga/ 5 rites/ etc.							
Other Forms of Exercise							

Weekly Supplements / Health Notes:

Weekly Song Selection
Week / /

1.
2.
3.
4.
5.

NOTES:

Raise Your Voice Diary
Week / /

	Mon.	Tues.	Wed.	Thurs.	Fri.	Sat.	Sun.
VSR							
Falsetto Upscale-							
Downscale-							
Transcending Tone Upscale-							
Downscale-							
Full Voice Upscale-							
Downscale-							
Vibrato Pitch, Larynx Stomach, Jaw							
Non-Vocal (Bullfrogs, Tongue Pushups)							
Advanced (Scream, Grit, Growl Whistle)							
Daily Dose							

Ultimate Breathing Workout Diary
Week / /

	Mon.	Tues.	Wed.	Thurs.	Fri.	Sat.	Sun.
Abdominal Release #1							
Abdominal Release #2							
Breath Capacity #1							
Breath Capacity #2							
Breath Release #1							
Breath Release #2							
Sustain #1							
Sustain #2							
Sustain #3							

Advanced Exercises:

Diet & Health
Week / /

	Mon.	Tues.	Wed.	Thurs.	Fri.	Sat.	Sun.
Cardio Jogging/ Swimming/ Rebounding/ Etc.							
Situps							
Yoga Flowfit/ Ashtanga/ 5 rites/ etc.							
Other Forms of Exercise							

Weekly Supplements / Health Notes:

The Ultimate Vocal Workout Diary

Weekly Song Selection
Week / /

1.
2.
3.
4.
5.

NOTES:

Raise Your Voice Diary
Week   /   /

	Mon.	Tues.	Wed.	Thurs.	Fri.	Sat.	Sun.
VSR							
Falsetto Upscale-							
Downscale-							
Transcending Tone Upscale-							
Downscale-							
Full Voice Upscale-							
Downscale-							
Vibrato Pitch, Larynx Stomach, Jaw							
Non-Vocal (Bullfrogs, Tongue Pushups)							
Advanced (Scream, Grit, Growl Whistle)							
Daily Dose							

Ultimate Breathing Workout Diary
Week / /

	Mon.	Tues.	Wed.	Thurs.	Fri.	Sat.	Sun.
Abdominal Release #1							
Abdominal Release #2							
Breath Capacity #1							
Breath Capacity #2							
Breath Release #1							
Breath Release #2							
Sustain #1							
Sustain #2							
Sustain #3							

Advanced Exercises:

_____
_____
_____
_____

Diet & Health
Week / /

	Mon.	Tues.	Wed.	Thurs.	Fri.	Sat.	Sun.
Cardio Jogging/ Swimming/ Rebounding/ Etc.							
Situps							
Yoga Flowfit/ Ashtanga/ 5 rites/ etc.							
Other Forms of Exercise							

Weekly Supplements / Health Notes:

Weekly Song Selection
Week / /

1.
2.
3.
4.
5.

NOTES:

Raise Your Voice Diary
Week / /

	Mon.	Tues.	Wed.	Thurs.	Fri.	Sat.	Sun.
VSR							
Falsetto Upscale-							
Downscale-							
Transcending Tone Upscale-							
Downscale-							
Full Voice Upscale-							
Downscale-							
Vibrato Pitch, Larynx Stomach, Jaw							
Non-Vocal (Bullfrogs, Tongue Pushups)							
Advanced (Scream, Grit, Growl Whistle)							
Daily Dose							

Ultimate Breathing Workout Diary
Week / /

	Mon.	Tues.	Wed.	Thurs.	Fri.	Sat.	Sun.
Abdominal Release #1							
Abdominal Release #2							
Breath Capacity #1							
Breath Capacity #2							
Breath Release #1							
Breath Release #2							
Sustain #1							
Sustain #2							
Sustain #3							

Advanced Exercises:

Diet & Health
Week / /

	Mon.	Tues.	Wed.	Thurs.	Fri.	Sat.	Sun.
Cardio Jogging/ Swimming/ Rebounding/ Etc.							
Situps							
Yoga Flowfit/ Ashtanga/ 5 rites/ etc.							
Other Forms of Exercise							

Weekly Supplements / Health Notes:

Weekly Song Selection
Week / /

1.
2.
3.
4.
5.

NOTES:

Raise Your Voice Diary
Week / /

	Mon.	Tues.	Wed.	Thurs.	Fri.	Sat.	Sun.
VSR							
Falsetto Upscale-							
Downscale-							
Transcending Tone Upscale-							
Downscale-							
Full Voice Upscale-							
Downscale-							
Vibrato Pitch, Larynx Stomach, Jaw							
Non-Vocal (Bullfrogs, Tongue Pushups)							
Advanced (Scream, Grit, Growl Whistle)							
Daily Dose							

Ultimate Breathing Workout Diary
Week / /

	Mon.	Tues.	Wed.	Thurs.	Fri.	Sat.	Sun.
Abdominal Release #1							
Abdominal Release #2							
Breath Capacity #1							
Breath Capacity #2							
Breath Release #1							
Breath Release #2							
Sustain #1							
Sustain #2							
Sustain #3							

Advanced Exercises:

Diet & Health
Week / /

	Mon.	Tues.	Wed.	Thurs.	Fri.	Sat.	Sun.
Cardio Jogging/ Swimming/ Rebounding/ Etc.							
Situps							
Yoga Flowfit/ Ashtanga/ 5 rites/ etc.							
Other Forms of Exercise							

Weekly Supplements / Health Notes:

Weekly Song Selection
Week / /

1.
2.
3.
4.
5.

NOTES:

Raise Your Voice Diary
Week   /   /

	Mon.	Tues.	Wed.	Thurs.	Fri.	Sat.	Sun.
VSR							
Falsetto Upscale-							
Downscale-							
Transcending Tone Upscale-							
Downscale-							
Full Voice Upscale-							
Downscale-							
Vibrato Pitch, Larynx Stomach, Jaw							
Non-Vocal (Bullfrogs, Tongue Pushups)							
Advanced (Scream, Grit, Growl Whistle)							
Daily Dose							

Ultimate Breathing Workout Diary
Week / /

	Mon.	Tues.	Wed.	Thurs.	Fri.	Sat.	Sun.
Abdominal Release #1							
Abdominal Release #2							
Breath Capacity #1							
Breath Capacity #2							
Breath Release #1							
Breath Release #2							
Sustain #1							
Sustain #2							
Sustain #3							

Advanced Exercises:

Diet & Health
Week / /

	Mon.	Tues.	Wed.	Thurs.	Fri.	Sat.	Sun.
Cardio Jogging/ Swimming/ Rebounding/ Etc.							
Situps							
Yoga Flowfit/ Ashtanga/ 5 rites/ etc.							
Other Forms of Exercise							

Weekly Supplements / Health Notes:

Weekly Song Selection
Week / /

1.
2.
3.
4.
5.

NOTES:

Raise Your Voice Diary
Week / /

	Mon.	Tues.	Wed.	Thurs.	Fri.	Sat.	Sun.
VSR							
Falsetto Upscale-							
Downscale-							
Transcending Tone Upscale-							
Downscale-							
Full Voice Upscale-							
Downscale-							
Vibrato Pitch, Larynx Stomach, Jaw							
Non-Vocal (Bullfrogs, Tongue Pushups)							
Advanced (Scream, Grit, Growl Whistle)							
Daily Dose							

Ultimate Breathing Workout Diary
Week   /   /

	Mon.	Tues.	Wed.	Thurs.	Fri.	Sat.	Sun.
Abdominal Release #1							
Abdominal Release #2							
Breath Capacity #1							
Breath Capacity #2							
Breath Release #1							
Breath Release #2							
Sustain #1							
Sustain #2							
Sustain #3							

Advanced Exercises:

Diet & Health
Week / /

	Mon.	Tues.	Wed.	Thurs.	Fri.	Sat.	Sun.
Cardio Jogging/ Swimming/ Rebounding/ Etc.							
Situps							
Yoga Flowfit/ Ashtanga/ 5 rites/ etc.							
Other Forms of Exercise							

Weekly Supplements / Health Notes:

Weekly Song Selection
Week / /

1.
2.
3.
4.
5.

NOTES:

Raise Your Voice Diary

Week / /

	Mon.	Tues.	Wed.	Thurs.	Fri.	Sat.	Sun.
VSR							
Falsetto Upscale-							
Downscale-							
Transcending Tone Upscale-							
Downscale-							
Full Voice Upscale-							
Downscale-							
Vibrato Pitch, Larynx Stomach, Jaw							
Non-Vocal (Bullfrogs, Tongue Pushups							
Advanced (Scream, Grit, Growl Whistle)							
Daily Dose							

Ultimate Breathing Workout Diary
Week   /   /

	Mon.	Tues.	Wed.	Thurs.	Fri.	Sat.	Sun.
Abdominal Release #1							
Abdominal Release #2							
Breath Capacity #1							
Breath Capacity #2							
Breath Release #1							
Breath Release #2							
Sustain #1							
Sustain #2							
Sustain #3							

Advanced Exercises:

Diet & Health
Week / /

	Mon.	Tues.	Wed.	Thurs.	Fri.	Sat.	Sun.
Cardio Jogging/ Swimming/ Rebounding/ Etc.							
Situps							
Yoga Flowfit/ Ashtanga/ 5 rites/ etc.							
Other Forms of Exercise							

Weekly Supplements / Health Notes:

Weekly Song Selection
Week / /

1. _____

2. _____

3. _____

4. _____

5. _____

NOTES:

Raise Your Voice Diary
Week / /

	Mon.	Tues.	Wed.	Thurs.	Fri.	Sat.	Sun.
VSR							
Falsetto Upscale-							
Downscale-							
Transcending Tone Upscale-							
Downscale-							
Full Voice Upscale-							
Downscale-							
Vibrato Pitch, Larynx Stomach, Jaw							
Non-Vocal (Bullfrogs, Tongue Pushups)							
Advanced (Scream, Grit, Growl Whistle)							
Daily Dose							

Ultimate Breathing Workout Diary
Week   /   /

	Mon.	Tues.	Wed.	Thurs.	Fri.	Sat.	Sun.
Abdominal Release #1							
Abdominal Release #2							
Breath Capacity #1							
Breath Capacity #2							
Breath Release #1							
Breath Release #2							
Sustain #1							
Sustain #2							
Sustain #3							

Advanced Exercises:

_____
_____
_____
_____

Diet & Health
Week / /

	Mon.	Tues.	Wed.	Thurs.	Fri.	Sat.	Sun.
Cardio Jogging/ Swimming/ Rebounding/ Etc.							
Situps							
Yoga Flowfit/ Ashtanga/ 5 rites/ etc.							
Other Forms of Exercise							

Weekly Supplements / Health Notes:

Weekly Song Selection
Week   /   /

1.
2.
3.
4.
5.

NOTES:

Raise Your Voice Diary
Week / /

	Mon.	Tues.	Wed.	Thurs.	Fri.	Sat.	Sun.
VSR							
Falsetto Upscale-							
Downscale-							
Transcending Tone Upscale-							
Downscale-							
Full Voice Upscale-							
Downscale-							
Vibrato Pitch, Larynx Stomach, Jaw							
Non-Vocal (Bullfrogs, Tongue Pushups)							
Advanced (Scream, Grit, Growl Whistle)							
Daily Dose							

Ultimate Breathing Workout Diary
Week   /   /

	Mon.	Tues.	Wed.	Thurs.	Fri.	Sat.	Sun.
Abdominal Release #1							
Abdominal Release #2							
Breath Capacity #1							
Breath Capacity #2							
Breath Release #1							
Breath Release #2							
Sustain #1							
Sustain #2							
Sustain #3							

Advanced Exercises:

Diet & Health
Week / /

	Mon.	Tues.	Wed.	Thurs.	Fri.	Sat.	Sun.
Cardio Jogging/ Swimming/ Rebounding/ Etc.							
Situps							
Yoga Flowfit/ Ashtanga/ 5 rites/ etc.							
Other Forms of Exercise							

Weekly Supplements / Health Notes:

Weekly Song Selection
Week   /   /

1.
2.
3.
4.
5.

NOTES:

Raise Your Voice Diary
Week / /

	Mon.	Tues.	Wed.	Thurs.	Fri.	Sat.	Sun.
VSR							
Falsetto Upscale-							
Downscale-							
Transcending Tone Upscale-							
Downscale-							
Full Voice Upscale-							
Downscale-							
Vibrato Pitch, Larynx Stomach, Jaw							
Non-Vocal (Bullfrogs, Tongue Pushups)							
Advanced (Scream, Grit, Growl Whistle)							
Daily Dose							

Ultimate Breathing Workout Diary
Week   /   /

	Mon.	Tues.	Wed.	Thurs.	Fri.	Sat.	Sun.
Abdominal Release #1							
Abdominal Release #2							
Breath Capacity #1							
Breath Capacity #2							
Breath Release #1							
Breath Release #2							
Sustain #1							
Sustain #2							
Sustain #3							

Advanced Exercises:

Diet & Health
Week / /

	Mon.	Tues.	Wed.	Thurs.	Fri.	Sat.	Sun.
Cardio Jogging/ Swimming/ Rebounding/ Etc.							
Situps							
Yoga Flowfit/ Ashtanga/ 5 rites/ etc.							
Other Forms of Exercise							

Weekly Supplements / Health Notes:

Weekly Song Selection
Week / /

1. _____

2. _____

3. _____

4. _____

5. _____

NOTES:

Raise Your Voice Diary
Week   /   /

	Mon.	Tues.	Wed.	Thurs.	Fri.	Sat.	Sun.
VSR							
Falsetto Upscale-							
Downscale-							
Transcending Tone Upscale-							
Downscale-							
Full Voice Upscale-							
Downscale-							
Vibrato Pitch, Larynx Stomach, Jaw							
Non-Vocal (Bullfrogs, Tongue Pushups)							
Advanced (Scream, Grit, Growl Whistle)							
Daily Dose							

Ultimate Breathing Workout Diary
Week   /   /

	Mon.	Tues.	Wed.	Thurs.	Fri.	Sat.	Sun.
Abdominal Release #1							
Abdominal Release #2							
Breath Capacity #1							
Breath Capacity #2							
Breath Release #1							
Breath Release #2							
Sustain #1							
Sustain #2							
Sustain #3							

Advanced Exercises:

Diet & Health
Week / /

	Mon.	Tues.	Wed.	Thurs.	Fri.	Sat.	Sun.
Cardio Jogging/ Swimming/ Rebounding/ Etc.							
Situps							
Yoga Flowfit/ Ashtanga/ 5 rites/ etc.							
Other Forms of Exercise							

Weekly Supplements / Health Notes:

Weekly Song Selection
Week / /

1.
2.
3.
4.
5.

NOTES:

Raise Your Voice Diary
Week / /

	Mon.	Tues.	Wed.	Thurs.	Fri.	Sat.	Sun.
VSR							
Falsetto Upscale-							
Downscale-							
Transcending Tone Upscale-							
Downscale-							
Full Voice Upscale-							
Downscale-							
Vibrato Pitch, Larynx Stomach, Jaw							
Non-Vocal (Bullfrogs, Tongue Pushups							
Advanced (Scream, Grit, Growl Whistle)							
Daily Dose							

Ultimate Breathing Workout Diary
Week / /

	Mon.	Tues.	Wed.	Thurs.	Fri.	Sat.	Sun.
Abdominal Release #1							
Abdominal Release #2							
Breath Capacity #1							
Breath Capacity #2							
Breath Release #1							
Breath Release #2							
Sustain #1							
Sustain #2							
Sustain #3							

Advanced Exercises:

Diet & Health
Week / /

	Mon.	Tues.	Wed.	Thurs.	Fri.	Sat.	Sun.
Cardio Jogging/ Swimming/ Rebounding/ Etc.							
Situps							
Yoga Flowfit/ Ashtanga/ 5 rites/ etc.							
Other Forms of Exercise							

Weekly Supplements / Health Notes:

Weekly Song Selection
Week   /   /

1.
2.
3.
4.
5.

NOTES:

Raise Your Voice Diary

Week / /

	Mon.	Tues.	Wed.	Thurs.	Fri.	Sat.	Sun.
VSR							
Falsetto Upscale-							
Downscale-							
Transcending Tone Upscale-							
Downscale-							
Full Voice Upscale-							
Downscale-							
Vibrato Pitch, Larynx Stomach, Jaw							
Non-Vocal (Bullfrogs, Tongue Pushups							
Advanced (Scream, Grit, Growl Whistle)							
Daily Dose							

Ultimate Breathing Workout Diary
Week   /   /

	Mon.	Tues.	Wed.	Thurs.	Fri.	Sat.	Sun.
Abdominal Release #1							
Abdominal Release #2							
Breath Capacity #1							
Breath Capacity #2							
Breath Release #1							
Breath Release #2							
Sustain #1							
Sustain #2							
Sustain #3							

Advanced Exercises:

Diet & Health
Week / /

	Mon.	Tues.	Wed.	Thurs.	Fri.	Sat.	Sun.
Cardio Jogging/ Swimming/ Rebounding/ Etc.							
Situps							
Yoga Flowfit/ Ashtanga/ 5 rites/ etc.							
Other Forms of Exercise							

Weekly Supplements / Health Notes:

118

Weekly Song Selection
Week / /

1. _____

2. _____

3. _____

4. _____

5. _____

NOTES:

Raise Your Voice Diary
Week / /

	Mon.	Tues.	Wed.	Thurs.	Fri.	Sat.	Sun.
VSR							
Falsetto Upscale-							
Downscale-							
Transcending Tone Upscale-							
Downscale-							
Full Voice Upscale-							
Downscale-							
Vibrato Pitch, Larynx Stomach, Jaw							
Non-Vocal (Bullfrogs, Tongue Pushups)							
Advanced (Scream, Grit, Growl Whistle)							
Daily Dose							

Ultimate Breathing Workout Diary
Week   /   /

	Mon.	Tues.	Wed.	Thurs.	Fri.	Sat.	Sun.
Abdominal Release #1							
Abdominal Release #2							
Breath Capacity #1							
Breath Capacity #2							
Breath Release #1							
Breath Release #2							
Sustain #1							
Sustain #2							
Sustain #3							

Advanced Exercises:

_____
_____
_____
_____

iet & Health
eek   /   /

	Mon.	Tues.	Wed.	Thurs.	Fri.	Sat.	Sun.
Cardio Jogging/ Swimming/ Rebounding/ Etc.							
Situps							
Yoga Flowfit/ Ashtanga/ 5 rites/ etc.							
Other Forms of Exercise							

Weekly Supplements / Health Notes:

The Ultimate Vocal Workout Diary

Weekly Song Selection
Week / /

1.
2.
3.
4.
5.

NOTES:

Raise Your Voice Diary
Week / /

	Mon.	Tues.	Wed.	Thurs.	Fri.	Sat.	Sun.
VSR							
Falsetto Upscale-							
Downscale-							
Transcending Tone Upscale-							
Downscale-							
Full Voice Upscale-							
Downscale-							
Vibrato Pitch, Larynx Stomach, Jaw							
Non-Vocal (Bullfrogs, Tongue Pushups							
Advanced (Scream, Grit, Growl Whistle)							
Daily Dose							

Ultimate Breathing Workout Diary
Week / /

	Mon.	Tues.	Wed.	Thurs.	Fri.	Sat.	Sun.
Abdominal Release #1							
Abdominal Release #2							
Breath Capacity #1							
Breath Capacity #2							
Breath Release #1							
Breath Release #2							
Sustain #1							
Sustain #2							
Sustain #3							

Advanced Exercises:

Diet & Health
Week / /

	Mon.	Tues.	Wed.	Thurs.	Fri.	Sat.	Sun.
Cardio Jogging/ Swimming/ Rebounding/ Etc.							
Situps							
Yoga Flowfit/ Ashtanga/ 5 rites/ etc.							
Other Forms of Exercise							

Weekly Supplements / Health Notes:

Weekly Song Selection
Week / /

1.
2.
3.
4.
5.

NOTES:

Raise Your Voice Diary
Week / /

	Mon.	Tues.	Wed.	Thurs.	Fri.	Sat.	Sun.
VSR							
Falsetto Upscale-							
Downscale-							
Transcending Tone Upscale-							
Downscale-							
Full Voice Upscale-							
Downscale-							
Vibrato Pitch, Larynx Stomach, Jaw							
Non-Vocal (Bullfrogs, Tongue Pushups							
Advanced (Scream, Grit, Growl Whistle)							
Daily Dose							

Ultimate Breathing Workout Diary
Week   /   /

	Mon.	Tues.	Wed.	Thurs.	Fri.	Sat.	Sun.
Abdominal Release #1							
Abdominal Release #2							
Breath Capacity #1							
Breath Capacity #2							
Breath Release #1							
Breath Release #2							
Sustain #1							
Sustain #2							
Sustain #3							

Advanced Exercises:

_____
_____
_____
_____

Diet & Health
Week / /

	Mon.	Tues.	Wed.	Thurs.	Fri.	Sat.	Sun.
Cardio Jogging/ Swimming/ Rebounding/ Etc.							
Situps							
Yoga Flowfit/ Ashtanga/ 5 rites/ etc.							
Other Forms of Exercise							

Weekly Supplements / Health Notes:

Weekly Song Selection
Week   /   /

1. _____

2. _____

3. _____

4. _____

5. _____

NOTES:

Raise Your Voice Diary
Week   /   /

	Mon.	Tues.	Wed.	Thurs.	Fri.	Sat.	Sun.
VSR							
Falsetto Upscale-							
Downscale-							
Transcending Tone Upscale-							
Downscale-							
Full Voice Upscale-							
Downscale-							
Vibrato Pitch, Larynx Stomach, Jaw							
Non-Vocal (Bullfrogs, Tongue Pushups)							
Advanced (Scream, Grit, Growl Whistle)							
Daily Dose							

Ultimate Breathing Workout Diary
Week / /

	Mon.	Tues.	Wed.	Thurs.	Fri.	Sat.	Sun.
Abdominal Release #1							
Abdominal Release #2							
Breath Capacity #1							
Breath Capacity #2							
Breath Release #1							
Breath Release #2							
Sustain #1							
Sustain #2							
Sustain #3							

Advanced Exercises:

_____
_____
_____
_____

Diet & Health
Week / /

	Mon.	Tues.	Wed.	Thurs.	Fri.	Sat.	Sun.
Cardio Jogging/ Swimming/ Rebounding/ Etc.							
Situps							
Yoga Flowfit/ Ashtanga/ 5 rites/ etc.							
Other Forms of Exercise							

Weekly Supplements / Health Notes:

Weekly Song Selection
Week / /

1.
2.
3.
4.
5.

NOTES:

Raise Your Voice Diary
Week / /

	Mon.	Tues.	Wed.	Thurs.	Fri.	Sat.	Sun.
VSR							
Falsetto Upscale-							
Downscale-							
Transcending Tone Upscale-							
Downscale-							
Full Voice Upscale-							
Downscale-							
Vibrato Pitch, Larynx Stomach, Jaw							
Non-Vocal (Bullfrogs, Tongue Pushups)							
Advanced (Scream, Grit, Growl Whistle)							
Daily Dose							

Ultimate Breathing Workout Diary
Week   /   /

	Mon.	Tues.	Wed.	Thurs.	Fri.	Sat.	Sun.
Abdominal Release #1							
Abdominal Release #2							
Breath Capacity #1							
Breath Capacity #2							
Breath Release #1							
Breath Release #2							
Sustain #1							
Sustain #2							
Sustain #3							

Advanced Exercises:

Diet & Health
Week / /

	Mon.	Tues.	Wed.	Thurs.	Fri.	Sat.	Sun.
Cardio Jogging/ Swimming/ Rebounding/ Etc.							
Situps							
Yoga Flowfit/ Ashtanga/ 5 rites/ etc.							
Other Forms of Exercise							

Weekly Supplements / Health Notes:

Weekly Song Selection
Week / /

1.
2.
3.
4.
5.

NOTES:

Raise Your Voice Diary
Week / /

	Mon.	Tues.	Wed.	Thurs.	Fri.	Sat.	Sun.
VSR							
Falsetto Upscale-							
Downscale-							
Transcending Tone Upscale-							
Downscale-							
Full Voice Upscale-							
Downscale-							
Vibrato Pitch, Larynx Stomach, Jaw							
Non-Vocal (Bullfrogs, Tongue Pushups							
Advanced (Scream, Grit, Growl Whistle)							
Daily Dose							

Ultimate Breathing Workout Diary
Week / /

	Mon.	Tues.	Wed.	Thurs.	Fri.	Sat.	Sun.
Abdominal Release #1							
Abdominal Release #2							
Breath Capacity #1							
Breath Capacity #2							
Breath Release #1							
Breath Release #2							
Sustain #1							
Sustain #2							
Sustain #3							

Advanced Exercises:

Diet & Health
Week / /

	Mon.	Tues.	Wed.	Thurs.	Fri.	Sat.	Sun.
Cardio Jogging/ Swimming/ Rebounding/ Etc.							
Situps							
Yoga Flowfit/ Ashtanga/ 5 rites/ etc.							
Other Forms of Exercise							

Weekly Supplements / Health Notes:

142 The Ultimate Vocal Workout Diary

Weekly Song Selection
Week   /   /

1. _____

2. _____

3. _____

4. _____

5. _____

NOTES:

Raise Your Voice Diary
Week / /

	Mon.	Tues.	Wed.	Thurs.	Fri.	Sat.	Sun.
VSR							
Falsetto Upscale-							
Downscale-							
Transcending Tone Upscale-							
Downscale-							
Full Voice Upscale-							
Downscale-							
Vibrato Pitch, Larynx Stomach, Jaw							
Non-Vocal (Bullfrogs, Tongue Pushups)							
Advanced (Scream, Grit, Growl Whistle)							
Daily Dose							

Ultimate Breathing Workout Diary
Week / /

	Mon.	Tues.	Wed.	Thurs.	Fri.	Sat.	Sun.
Abdominal Release #1							
Abdominal Release #2							
Breath Capacity #1							
Breath Capacity #2							
Breath Release #1							
Breath Release #2							
Sustain #1							
Sustain #2							
Sustain #3							

Advanced Exercises:

_____
_____
_____
_____

Diet & Health
Week / /

	Mon.	Tues.	Wed.	Thurs.	Fri.	Sat.	Sun.
Cardio Jogging/ Swimming/ Rebounding/ Etc.							
Situps							
Yoga Flowfit/ Ashtanga/ 5 rites/ etc.							
Other Forms of Exercise							

Weekly Supplements / Health Notes:

_____
_____
_____
_____
_____
_____
_____
_____
_____
_____

Weekly Song Selection
Week / /

1.
2.
3.
4.
5.

NOTES:

Raise Your Voice Diary
Week   /   /

	Mon.	Tues.	Wed.	Thurs.	Fri.	Sat.	Sun.
VSR							
Falsetto Upscale-							
Downscale-							
Transcending Tone Upscale-							
Downscale-							
Full Voice Upscale-							
Downscale-							
Vibrato Pitch, Larynx Stomach, Jaw							
Non-Vocal (Bullfrogs, Tongue Pushups							
Advanced (Scream, Grit, Growl Whistle)							
Daily Dose							

Ultimate Breathing Workout Diary
Week   /   /

	Mon.	Tues.	Wed.	Thurs.	Fri.	Sat.	Sun.
Abdominal Release #1							
Abdominal Release #2							
Breath Capacity #1							
Breath Capacity #2							
Breath Release #1							
Breath Release #2							
Sustain #1							
Sustain #2							
Sustain #3							

Advanced Exercises:

Diet & Health
Week / /

	Mon.	Tues.	Wed.	Thurs.	Fri.	Sat.	Sun.
Cardio Jogging/ Swimming/ Rebounding/ Etc.							
Situps							
Yoga Flowfit/ Ashtanga/ 5 rites/ etc.							
Other Forms of Exercise							

Weekly Supplements / Health Notes:

Weekly Song Selection
Week   /   /

1.

2.

3.

4.

5.

NOTES:

Raise Your Voice Diary
Week / /

	Mon.	Tues.	Wed.	Thurs.	Fri.	Sat.	Sun.
VSR							
Falsetto Upscale-							
Downscale-							
Transcending Tone Upscale-							
Downscale-							
Full Voice Upscale-							
Downscale-							
Vibrato Pitch, Larynx Stomach, Jaw							
Non-Vocal (Bullfrogs, Tongue Pushups)							
Advanced (Scream, Grit, Growl Whistle)							
Daily Dose							

Ultimate Breathing Workout Diary
Week   /   /

	Mon.	Tues.	Wed.	Thurs.	Fri.	Sat.	Sun.
Abdominal Release #1							
Abdominal Release #2							
Breath Capacity #1							
Breath Capacity #2							
Breath Release #1							
Breath Release #2							
Sustain #1							
Sustain #2							
Sustain #3							

Advanced Exercises:

Diet & Health
Week / /

	Mon.	Tues.	Wed.	Thurs.	Fri.	Sat.	Sun.
Cardio Jogging/ Swimming/ Rebounding/ Etc.							
Situps							
Yoga Flowfit/ Ashtanga/ 5 rites/ etc.							
Other Forms of Exercise							

Weekly Supplements / Health Notes:

Weekly Song Selection
Week   /   /

1.
2.
3.
4.
5.

NOTES:

Raise Your Voice Diary
Week / /

	Mon.	Tues.	Wed.	Thurs.	Fri.	Sat.	Sun.
VSR							
Falsetto Upscale-							
Downscale-							
Transcending Tone Upscale-							
Downscale-							
Full Voice Upscale-							
Downscale-							
Vibrato Pitch, Larynx Stomach, Jaw							
Non-Vocal (Bullfrogs, Tongue Pushups)							
Advanced (Scream, Grit, Growl Whistle)							
Daily Dose							

Ultimate Breathing Workout Diary
Week / /

	Mon.	Tues.	Wed.	Thurs.	Fri.	Sat.	Sun.
Abdominal Release #1							
Abdominal Release #2							
Breath Capacity #1							
Breath Capacity #2							
Breath Release #1							
Breath Release #2							
Sustain #1							
Sustain #2							
Sustain #3							

Advanced Exercises:

_____
_____
_____
_____
_____

Diet & Health
Week / /

	Mon.	Tues.	Wed.	Thurs.	Fri.	Sat.	Sun.
Cardio Jogging/ Swimming/ Rebounding/ Etc.							
Situps							
Yoga Flowfit/ Ashtanga/ 5 rites/ etc.							
Other Forms of Exercise							

Weekly Supplements / Health Notes:

Weekly Song Selection
Week / /

1.
2.
3.
4.
5.

NOTES:

Raise Your Voice Diary
Week   /   /

	Mon.	Tues.	Wed.	Thurs.	Fri.	Sat.	Sun.
VSR							
Falsetto Upscale-							
Downscale-							
Transcending Tone Upscale-							
Downscale-							
Full Voice Upscale-							
Downscale-							
Vibrato Pitch, Larynx Stomach, Jaw							
Non-Vocal (Bullfrogs, Tongue Pushups)							
Advanced (Scream, Grit, Growl Whistle)							
Daily Dose							

Ultimate Breathing Workout Diary
Week / /

	Mon.	Tues.	Wed.	Thurs.	Fri.	Sat.	Sun.
Abdominal Release #1							
Abdominal Release #2							
Breath Capacity #1							
Breath Capacity #2							
Breath Release #1							
Breath Release #2							
Sustain #1							
Sustain #2							
Sustain #3							

Advanced Exercises:

_____
_____
_____
_____

Diet & Health
Week / /

	Mon.	Tues.	Wed.	Thurs.	Fri.	Sat.	Sun.
Cardio Jogging/ Swimming/ Rebounding/ Etc.							
Situps							
Yoga Flowfit/ Ashtanga/ 5 rites/ etc.							
Other Forms of Exercise							

Weekly Supplements / Health Notes:

Weekly Song Selection
Week / /

1. _____
2. _____
3. _____
4. _____
5. _____

NOTES:

_____
_____
_____
_____
_____
_____
_____
_____
_____
_____
_____
_____
_____
_____
_____
_____
_____
_____
_____
_____

Raise Your Voice Diary
Week / /

	Mon.	Tues.	Wed.	Thurs.	Fri.	Sat.	Sun.
VSR							
Falsetto Upscale-							
Downscale-							
Transcending Tone Upscale-							
Downscale-							
Full Voice Upscale-							
Downscale-							
Vibrato Pitch, Larynx Stomach, Jaw							
Non-Vocal (Bullfrogs, Tongue Pushups)							
Advanced (Scream, Grit, Growl Whistle)							
Daily Dose							

Ultimate Breathing Workout Diary
Week / /

	Mon.	Tues.	Wed.	Thurs.	Fri.	Sat.	Sun.
Abdominal Release #1							
Abdominal Release #2							
Breath Capacity #1							
Breath Capacity #2							
Breath Release #1							
Breath Release #2							
Sustain #1							
Sustain #2							
Sustain #3							

Advanced Exercises:

Diet & Health
Week / /

	Mon.	Tues.	Wed.	Thurs.	Fri.	Sat.	Sun.
Cardio Jogging/ Swimming/ Rebounding/ Etc.							
Situps							
Yoga Flowfit/ Ashtanga/ 5 rites/ etc.							
Other Forms of Exercise							

Weekly Supplements / Health Notes:

_____
_____
_____
_____
_____
_____
_____
_____
_____
_____
_____
_____

Weekly Song Selection
Week / /

1.
2.
3.
4.
5.

NOTES:

Raise Your Voice Diary
Week / /

	Mon.	Tues.	Wed.	Thurs.	Fri.	Sat.	Sun.
VSR							
Falsetto Upscale-							
Downscale-							
Transcending Tone Upscale-							
Downscale-							
Full Voice Upscale-							
Downscale-							
Vibrato Pitch, Larynx Stomach, Jaw							
Non-Vocal (Bullfrogs, Tongue Pushups)							
Advanced (Scream, Grit, Growl Whistle)							
Daily Dose							

Ultimate Breathing Workout Diary
Week   /   /

	Mon.	Tues.	Wed.	Thurs.	Fri.	Sat.	Sun.
Abdominal Release #1							
Abdominal Release #2							
Breath Capacity #1							
Breath Capacity #2							
Breath Release #1							
Breath Release #2							
Sustain #1							
Sustain #2							
Sustain #3							

Advanced Exercises:

Diet & Health
Week / /

	Mon.	Tues.	Wed.	Thurs.	Fri.	Sat.	Sun.
Cardio Jogging/ Swimming/ Rebounding/ Etc.							
Situps							
Yoga Flowfit/ Ashtanga/ 5 rites/ etc.							
Other Forms of Exercise							

Weekly Supplements / Health Notes:

_____
_____
_____
_____
_____
_____
_____
_____
_____
_____
_____
_____

Weekly Song Selection
Week / /

1. _____

2. _____

3. _____

4. _____

5. _____

NOTES:

Raise Your Voice Diary
Week   /   /

	Mon.	Tues.	Wed.	Thurs.	Fri.	Sat.	Sun.
VSR							
Falsetto Upscale-							
Downscale-							
Transcending Tone Upscale-							
Downscale-							
Full Voice Upscale-							
Downscale-							
Vibrato Pitch, Larynx Stomach, Jaw							
Non-Vocal (Bullfrogs, Tongue Pushups)							
Advanced (Scream, Grit, Growl Whistle)							
Daily Dose							

Ultimate Breathing Workout Diary
Week / /

	Mon.	Tues.	Wed.	Thurs.	Fri.	Sat.	Sun.
Abdominal Release #1							
Abdominal Release #2							
Breath Capacity #1							
Breath Capacity #2							
Breath Release #1							
Breath Release #2							
Sustain #1							
Sustain #2							
Sustain #3							

Advanced Exercises:

Diet & Health
Week / /

	Mon.	Tues.	Wed.	Thurs.	Fri.	Sat.	Sun.
Cardio Jogging/ Swimming/ Rebounding/ Etc.							
Situps							
Yoga Flowfit/ Ashtanga/ 5 rites/ etc.							
Other Forms of Exercise							

Weekly Supplements / Health Notes:

Weekly Song Selection
Week / /

1. _____

2. _____

3. _____

4. _____

5. _____

NOTES:

Raise Your Voice Diary
Week / /

	Mon.	Tues.	Wed.	Thurs.	Fri.	Sat.	Sun.
VSR							
Falsetto Upscale-							
Downscale-							
Transcending Tone Upscale-							
Downscale-							
Full Voice Upscale-							
Downscale-							
Vibrato Pitch, Larynx Stomach, Jaw							
Non-Vocal (Bullfrogs, Tongue Pushups)							
Advanced (Scream, Grit, Growl Whistle)							
Daily Dose							

Ultimate Breathing Workout Diary
Week / /

	Mon.	Tues.	Wed.	Thurs.	Fri.	Sat.	Sun.
Abdominal Release #1							
Abdominal Release #2							
Breath Capacity #1							
Breath Capacity #2							
Breath Release #1							
Breath Release #2							
Sustain #1							
Sustain #2							
Sustain #3							

Advanced Exercises:

Diet & Health
Week / /

	Mon.	Tues.	Wed.	Thurs.	Fri.	Sat.	Sun.
Cardio Jogging/ Swimming/ Rebounding/ Etc.							
Situps							
Yoga Flowfit/ Ashtanga/ 5 rites/ etc.							
Other Forms of Exercise							

Weekly Supplements / Health Notes:

Weekly Song Selection
Week   /   /

1.
2.
3.
4.
5.

NOTES:

Raise Your Voice Diary
Week   /   /

	Mon.	Tues.	Wed.	Thurs.	Fri.	Sat.	Sun.
VSR							
Falsetto Upscale-							
Downscale-							
Transcending Tone Upscale-							
Downscale-							
Full Voice Upscale-							
Downscale-							
Vibrato Pitch, Larynx Stomach, Jaw							
Non-Vocal (Bullfrogs, Tongue Pushups)							
Advanced (Scream, Grit, Growl Whistle)							
Daily Dose							

Ultimate Breathing Workout Diary
Week   /   /

	Mon.	Tues.	Wed.	Thurs.	Fri.	Sat.	Sun.
Abdominal Release #1							
Abdominal Release #2							
Breath Capacity #1							
Breath Capacity #2							
Breath Release #1							
Breath Release #2							
Sustain #1							
Sustain #2							
Sustain #3							

Advanced Exercises:

Diet & Health

Week / /

	Mon.	Tues.	Wed.	Thurs.	Fri.	Sat.	Sun.
Cardio Jogging/ Swimming/ Rebounding/ Etc.							
Situps							
Yoga Flowfit/ Ashtanga/ 5 rites/ etc.							
Other Forms of Exercise							

Weekly Supplements / Health Notes:

Weekly Song Selection
Week / /

1.
2.
3.
4.
5.

NOTES:

Raise Your Voice Diary
Week   /   /

	Mon.	Tues.	Wed.	Thurs.	Fri.	Sat.	Sun.
VSR							
Falsetto Upscale-							
Downscale-							
Transcending Tone Upscale-							
Downscale-							
Full Voice Upscale-							
Downscale-							
Vibrato Pitch, Larynx Stomach, Jaw							
Non-Vocal (Bullfrogs, Tongue Pushups)							
Advanced (Scream, Grit, Growl Whistle)							
Daily Dose							

Ultimate Breathing Workout Diary
Week / /

	Mon.	Tues.	Wed.	Thurs.	Fri.	Sat.	Sun.
Abdominal Release #1							
Abdominal Release #2							
Breath Capacity #1							
Breath Capacity #2							
Breath Release #1							
Breath Release #2							
Sustain #1							
Sustain #2							
Sustain #3							

Advanced Exercises:

_____
_____
_____
_____

Diet & Health
Week / /

	Mon.	Tues.	Wed.	Thurs.	Fri.	Sat.	Sun.
Cardio Jogging/ Swimming/ Rebounding/ Etc.							
Situps							
Yoga Flowfit/ Ashtanga/ 5 rites/ etc.							
Other Forms of Exercise							

Weekly Supplements / Health Notes:

Weekly Song Selection
Week / /

1.
2.
3.
4.
5.

NOTES:

Raise Your Voice Diary
Week / /

	Mon.	Tues.	Wed.	Thurs.	Fri.	Sat.	Sun.
VSR							
Falsetto Upscale-							
Downscale-							
Transcending Tone Upscale-							
Downscale-							
Full Voice Upscale-							
Downscale-							
Vibrato Pitch, Larynx Stomach, Jaw							
Non-Vocal (Bullfrogs, Tongue Pushups							
Advanced (Scream, Grit, Growl Whistle)							
Daily Dose							

Ultimate Breathing Workout Diary
Week   /   /

	Mon.	Tues.	Wed.	Thurs.	Fri.	Sat.	Sun.
Abdominal Release #1							
Abdominal Release #2							
Breath Capacity #1							
Breath Capacity #2							
Breath Release #1							
Breath Release #2							
Sustain #1							
Sustain #2							
Sustain #3							

Advanced Exercises:

Diet & Health
Week / /

	Mon.	Tues.	Wed.	Thurs.	Fri.	Sat.	Sun.
Cardio Jogging/ Swimming/ Rebounding/ Etc.							
Situps							
Yoga Flowfit/ Ashtanga/ 5 rites/ etc.							
Other Forms of Exercise							

Weekly Supplements / Health Notes:

The Ultimate Vocal Workout Diary

Weekly Song Selection
Week   / /

1.
2.
3.
4.
5.

NOTES:

Raise Your Voice Diary
Week / /

	Mon.	Tues.	Wed.	Thurs.	Fri.	Sat.	Sun.
VSR							
Falsetto Upscale-							
Downscale-							
Transcending Tone Upscale-							
Downscale-							
Full Voice Upscale-							
Downscale-							
Vibrato Pitch, Larynx Stomach, Jaw							
Non-Vocal (Bullfrogs, Tongue Pushups)							
Advanced (Scream, Grit, Growl Whistle)							
Daily Dose							

Ultimate Breathing Workout Diary
Week / /

	Mon.	Tues.	Wed.	Thurs.	Fri.	Sat.	Sun.
Abdominal Release #1							
Abdominal Release #2							
Breath Capacity #1							
Breath Capacity #2							
Breath Release #1							
Breath Release #2							
Sustain #1							
Sustain #2							
Sustain #3							

Advanced Exercises:

_____
_____
_____

Diet & Health
Week / /

	Mon.	Tues.	Wed.	Thurs.	Fri.	Sat.	Sun.
Cardio Jogging/ Swimming/ Rebounding/ Etc.							
Situps							
Yoga Flowfit/ Ashtanga/ 5 rites/ etc.							
Other Forms of Exercise							

Weekly Supplements / Health Notes:

The Ultimate Vocal Workout Diary

Weekly Song Selection
Week / /

1.
2.
3.
4.
5.

NOTES:

Raise Your Voice Diary
Week   /   /

	Mon.	Tues.	Wed.	Thurs.	Fri.	Sat.	Sun.
VSR							
Falsetto Upscale-							
Downscale-							
Transcending Tone Upscale-							
Downscale-							
Full Voice Upscale-							
Downscale-							
Vibrato Pitch, Larynx Stomach, Jaw							
Non-Vocal (Bullfrogs, Tongue Pushups							
Advanced (Scream, Grit, Growl Whistle)							
Daily Dose							

Ultimate Breathing Workout Diary
Week   /   /

	Mon.	Tues.	Wed.	Thurs.	Fri.	Sat.	Sun.
Abdominal Release #1							
Abdominal Release #2							
Breath Capacity #1							
Breath Capacity #2							
Breath Release #1							
Breath Release #2							
Sustain #1							
Sustain #2							
Sustain #3							

Advanced Exercises:

_____

_____

_____

_____

Diet & Health
Week / /

	Mon.	Tues.	Wed.	Thurs.	Fri.	Sat.	Sun.
Cardio Jogging/ Swimming/ Rebounding/ Etc.							
Situps							
Yoga Flowfit/ Ashtanga/ 5 rites/ etc.							
Other Forms of Exercise							

Weekly Supplements / Health Notes:

Weekly Song Selection
Week / /

1.
2.
3.
4.
5.

NOTES:

Raise Your Voice Diary
Week   /   /

	Mon.	Tues.	Wed.	Thurs.	Fri.	Sat.	Sun.
VSR							
Falsetto Upscale-							
Downscale-							
Transcending Tone Upscale-							
Downscale-							
Full Voice Upscale-							
Downscale-							
Vibrato Pitch, Larynx Stomach, Jaw							
Non-Vocal (Bullfrogs, Tongue Pushups)							
Advanced (Scream, Grit, Growl Whistle)							
Daily Dose							

Ultimate Breathing Workout Diary
Week   /   /

	Mon.	Tues.	Wed.	Thurs.	Fri.	Sat.	Sun.
Abdominal Release #1							
Abdominal Release #2							
Breath Capacity #1							
Breath Capacity #2							
Breath Release #1							
Breath Release #2							
Sustain #1							
Sustain #2							
Sustain #3							

Advanced Exercises:

_____
_____
_____
_____

Diet & Health
Week / /

	Mon.	Tues.	Wed.	Thurs.	Fri.	Sat.	Sun.
Cardio Jogging/ Swimming/ Rebounding/ Etc.							
Situps							
Yoga Flowfit/ Ashtanga/ 5 rites/ etc.							
Other Forms of Exercise							

Weekly Supplements / Health Notes:

Weekly Song Selection
Week / /

1. _____

2. _____

3. _____

4. _____

5. _____

NOTES:

Raise Your Voice Diary
Week   /   /

	Mon.	Tues.	Wed.	Thurs.	Fri.	Sat.	Sun.
VSR							
Falsetto Upscale-							
Downscale-							
Transcending Tone Upscale-							
Downscale-							
Full Voice Upscale-							
Downscale-							
Vibrato Pitch, Larynx Stomach, Jaw							
Non-Vocal (Bullfrogs, Tongue Pushups)							
Advanced (Scream, Grit, Growl Whistle)							
Daily Dose							

Ultimate Breathing Workout Diary
Week   /   /

	Mon.	Tues.	Wed.	Thurs.	Fri.	Sat.	Sun.
Abdominal Release #1							
Abdominal Release #2							
Breath Capacity #1							
Breath Capacity #2							
Breath Release #1							
Breath Release #2							
Sustain #1							
Sustain #2							
Sustain #3							

Advanced Exercises:

Diet & Health
Week / /

	Mon.	Tues.	Wed.	Thurs.	Fri.	Sat.	Sun.
Cardio Jogging/ Swimming/ Rebounding/ Etc.							
Situps							
Yoga Flowfit/ Ashtanga/ 5 rites/ etc.							
Other Forms of Exercise							

Weekly Supplements / Health Notes:

Weekly Song Selection
Week   /   /

1.

2.

3.

4.

5.

NOTES:

Raise Your Voice Diary
Week   /   /

	Mon.	Tues.	Wed.	Thurs.	Fri.	Sat.	Sun.
VSR							
Falsetto Upscale-							
Downscale-							
Transcending Tone Upscale-							
Downscale-							
Full Voice Upscale-							
Downscale-							
Vibrato Pitch, Larynx Stomach, Jaw							
Non-Vocal (Bullfrogs, Tongue Pushups)							
Advanced (Scream, Grit, Growl Whistle)							
Daily Dose							

Ultimate Breathing Workout Diary
Week   /   /

	Mon.	Tues.	Wed.	Thurs.	Fri.	Sat.	Sun.
Abdominal Release #1							
Abdominal Release #2							
Breath Capacity #1							
Breath Capacity #2							
Breath Release #1							
Breath Release #2							
Sustain #1							
Sustain #2							
Sustain #3							

Advanced Exercises:

Diet & Health
Week   /   /

	Mon.	Tues.	Wed.	Thurs.	Fri.	Sat.	Sun.
Cardio Jogging/ Swimming/ Rebounding/ Etc.							
Situps							
Yoga Flowfit/ Ashtanga/ 5 rites/ etc.							
Other Forms of Exercise							

Weekly Supplements / Health Notes:

Weekly Song Selection
Week / /

1.
2.
3.
4.
5.

NOTES:

Raise Your Voice Diary
Week / /

	Mon.	Tues.	Wed.	Thurs.	Fri.	Sat.	Sun.
VSR							
Falsetto Upscale-							
Downscale-							
Transcending Tone Upscale-							
Downscale-							
Full Voice Upscale-							
Downscale-							
Vibrato Pitch, Larynx Stomach, Jaw							
Non-Vocal (Bullfrogs, Tongue Pushups)							
Advanced (Scream, Grit, Growl Whistle)							
Daily Dose							

Ultimate Breathing Workout Diary
Week   /   /

	Mon.	Tues.	Wed.	Thurs.	Fri.	Sat.	Sun.
Abdominal Release #1							
Abdominal Release #2							
Breath Capacity #1							
Breath Capacity #2							
Breath Release #1							
Breath Release #2							
Sustain #1							
Sustain #2							
Sustain #3							

Advanced Exercises:

Diet & Health
Week / /

	Mon.	Tues.	Wed.	Thurs.	Fri.	Sat.	Sun.
Cardio Jogging/ Swimming/ Rebounding/ Etc.							
Situps							
Yoga Flowfit/ Ashtanga/ 5 rites/ etc.							
Other Forms of Exercise							

Weekly Supplements / Health Notes:

Weekly Song Selection
Week / /

1.
2.
3.
4.
5.

NOTES:

Raise Your Voice Diary
Week   /   /

	Mon.	Tues.	Wed.	Thurs.	Fri.	Sat.	Sun.
VSR							
Falsetto Upscale-							
Downscale-							
Transcending Tone Upscale-							
Downscale-							
Full Voice Upscale-							
Downscale-							
Vibrato Pitch, Larynx Stomach, Jaw							
Non-Vocal (Bullfrogs, Tongue Pushups)							
Advanced (Scream, Grit, Growl Whistle)							
Daily Dose							

Ultimate Breathing Workout Diary
Week / /

	Mon.	Tues.	Wed.	Thurs.	Fri.	Sat.	Sun.
Abdominal Release #1							
Abdominal Release #2							
Breath Capacity #1							
Breath Capacity #2							
Breath Release #1							
Breath Release #2							
Sustain #1							
Sustain #2							
Sustain #3							

Advanced Exercises:

Diet & Health
Week / /

	Mon.	Tues.	Wed.	Thurs.	Fri.	Sat.	Sun.
Cardio Jogging/ Swimming/ Rebounding/ Etc.							
Situps							
Yoga Flowfit/ Ashtanga/ 5 rites/ etc.							
Other Forms of Exercise							

Weekly Supplements / Health Notes:

Weekly Song Selection
Week / /

1.
2.
3.
4.
5.

NOTES:

www.ingramcontent.com/pod-product-compliance
Lightning Source LLC
Chambersburg PA
CBHW070602100426
42744CB00006B/380